D ear Reader,
Welcome to the world of safeguarding spaces and entrepreneurial dreams! This book is your guiding light into the realms of CCTV installation Job and the journey of starting your own business.

Are you ready to dive into the world of security cameras? Imagine yourself, step by step, connecting wires, positioning cameras, and creating a shield of protection. This book holds your hand through this process, making it as simple as following a recipe in the kitchen.

But it's not just about setting up cameras , it's about turning this skill into a Job or Business. From crafting a plan to market your services, this guide walks you through the entire process. Whether you're just starting or have some experience, this book is designed for both beginners and field technicians.

Consider this book as your friendly mentor, patiently explaining each step. It's not just a book; it's a friend accompanying you on this exciting journey of turning your passion into a thriving Job or Business.

So, let's embark on this adventure together, exploring the world of CCTV installation and entrepreneurship!Best wishes,
Ali Ansari

CCTV Secret & Entrepreneurship
By : Ali Ansari

The Cover
By : Shaikh Kishore

First Edition - August 2024
Price: INR: 360/- Only

Copyright Disclaimer:

Published by
Silicon Corporation
Balarampur , Purulia , West Bengal

TABLE OF CONTENTS

Chapter 1: Introduction to CCTV Technology
Chapter 2: Components & Tools
Chapter 3: CCTV Infrastructure System Design
Chapter 4: Machine, Hard Disk & Cable Selection
Chapter 5: Installation and Configuration
Chapter 6: Video Analytics and Advanced Features
Chapter 7: Network & Mobile View Configuration
Chapter 8: Live Project Hand on Practices
Chapter 9: Troubleshooting and Maintenance
Chapter 10: Basic of Marketing & Sales for Entrepreneur

Chapter 1

Introduction to CCTV Technology

- ◦ **Overview of CCTV and Objects**
- ◦ **Evolution of CCTV technology**
- ◦ **Types of CCTV system**

OVERVIEW OF CCTV AND ITS OBJECTS

CCTV stands for Closed-Circuit Television. It refers to a system in which video cameras transmit signals to a specific set of monitors, unlike broadcast television.

The primary goal of CCTV is to monitor and capture video footage for various purposes, including security, surveillance, and process monitoring & Audio also Storage in hard disk.

USES OF CCTV CAMERAS

Security Surveillance:

- · **CCTV is extensively used for security purposes in Government ,public spaces, businesses, and residential areas.**
- · **Helps detect criminal activities and provides evidence in case of incidents.**

Traffic Monitoring:

- Used for managing traffic flow, monitoring intersections, and enhancing road safety.
- Enables authorities to respond quickly to traffic incidents .

Commercial Establishments:

- Businesses use CCTV to prevent theft, monitor employee activities, and ensure workplace safety.
- Acts as a deterrent against internal and external threats .

Public Spaces:

- CCTV is deployed in public places like parks, malls, and transport hubs to enhance public safety.
- Aids in crowd management and emergency response.

Process Monitoring:

- Industries use CCTV to monitor manufacturing processes, ensuring quality control and safety.
- Helpful in identifying and addressing issues in real-time.

Home Security:

- Increasingly popular for residential security. Allows homeowners to monitor their property remotely and receive alerts in case of suspicious activities.

Evolution of CCTV technology

Phase I

The first ever documented use of a CCTV Camera traces back to Germany in the year 1942. This was the World War II era and the Germans used cameras to observe the firing of rockets. German scientists placed cameras inside boxes and observed the launches of A4 missiles.

Monitors and cameras were the only two components in this

architecture and this lacked the ability to record events for personnel to view later. Only live monitoring of footage was possible.

Phase II

While there was no major evolution in CCTV surveillance cameras post the 40s, the next major breakthrough was in the 60s. This was when multiple cameras could be connected together to a single monitor and the introduction of a switch box allowed users to alternate between multiple cameras on one monitor to surveillance areas. However, only one camera could be viewed at once time.

In the 70s, additional systems such as solid state cameras, VCRs and multiplexers were introduced in the market. These three systems put CCTV technology on a sophisticated pedestal with each contributing to the evolution of its architecture.

While solid state cameras improved the overall quality and reliability of cameras, multiplexers enabled users to view multiple cameras at once on a single monitor through split screen. The biggest value addition at this time was the integration of VCR technology, which allowed people to record footage and monitor them later.

This meant that human intervention could be cut off from the architecture significantly and that the footage from recordings could be used as evidence in judicial proceedings.

Phase III

Despite being revolutionary, this ecosystem of surveillance technology was not without its fair share of disadvantages. For example, the quality of recorded footage was very poor with grains and low resolution. This made its application in law and order ineffective because no solid conclusions could be drawn from the footage due to unclear video quality.

Also, the VCR technology was temperamental by itself as

operators could only either view a recording or monitor surroundings at once. They couldn't do both simultaneously.

To fix most of these concerns arrived Digital Video Recording technology. Also known as DVR, this digitized the recording and surveillance process. With DVR, the video quality was much better at higher resolutions and it removed what was the biggest obstacle in the architecture – recording tapes getting over or their need to be constantly replaced.

Technically, DVR systems had multiplexers embedded in them. This reduced the number of equipment from two to one. Next, storage was no longer reliant on video tapes but digital drives that offered more space for footage and automatic deletion after a specific time. The more the storage space, the longer the recording duration.

The DVR technology was completely automated and required no manual interference. For instance, it allowed operators to view recorded footage and monitor the real world simultaneously, get details on the date and time of events and more.

Besides, IP-enabled systems went a step ahead and let users view and even operate cameras from remote. With a stable internet connection, high-resolution footage or images could be transmitted to and from anywhere.

Phase IV

The current generation of CCTV technology is far more advanced than its predecessors. We call them PTZ or Pan, Tilt and Zoom. Some of the standout features of this architecture are that they deploy multiple lenses in cameras for clarity and purposes (such as night vision), audio can be recorded in real time, surveillance could even transmit audio and question trespassers or intruders through the camera and get their response in real time and more.

Besides, recorded footage could be panned, zoomed and tilted for better viewing and facial recognition purposes.

TYPES OF CCTV SYSTEM

HD Camera

Superior quality (HD) CCTV surveillance cameras satisfy the requirement for high goal imaging, fundamental for the majority reconnaissance purposes. Guaranteeing the nature of video film is of an adequate standard that can be utilized both for precaution security reconnaissance and for proof purposes.

Features

- Cost effective (Affordable for general public or small business owner)
- Maintenance required : Yearly basis
- Parts price: Normal / Affordable
- Durability: 3-5 years approx.
- Resolution: VGA to 5 MP
- Easy installation

IP CCTV

IP denote Internet Protocol, an IP camera is a digital video camera that sends and receives image data over an IP network. They are often used for surveillance, but unlike analog closed-circuit television (CCTV) cameras, they don't need a local recording device.

IP (Internet Protocol) CCTV systems transmit data over computer networks, offering digital clarity. Cameras can be connected to the internet for remote access and control.

Features

- Expensive than HD
- Low Maintenance Cost
- Parts price : High
- Durability: 5 + years approx.
- Resolution: 2.0 to 16 MP

- Upgraded picture quality.
- Further developed distinguishing proof capacities .
- Knowledge & Skills required for installation .

Wireless camera

Remote surveillance cameras are shut circuit TV (CCTV) cameras that communicate a video and sound transmission to a remote beneficiary through a radio band.

Features

- Wireless camera .
- Affordable for general public .
- Low Maintenance .
- Durability: 3+ year approx.
- Resolution : VGA to 5 MP.

C- Mount Camera

A   C-Mount CCTV (Shut Circuit TV) camera is a kind of observation camera framework that uses a C-Mount focal point interface, considering exchangeable focal points to be joined to the camera. The "C-Mount" alludes to the normalized screw string type and distance between the focal point and the camera sensor, empowering adaptability in focal point determination to suit different observing requirements.

These cameras are usually utilized in security frameworks, modern checking, and logical applications because of their versatility. C-Mount CCTV cameras regularly offer higher goal and further developed picture quality, considering definite observation film, and the capacity to utilize various focal points awards adaptability in catching different perspectives, including significant distance, wide-point, or zoomed-in shots.

Features

- Tradable focal points: C-Mount cameras can utilize various focal points in view of explicit observation needs.
- Adaptability: These cameras offer adaptability in catching different perspectives, like wide-point or zoomed-in shots.
- High goal: They frequently give higher goal to more clear and point by point reconnaissance film.
- Normalized plan: The normalized C-Mount interface takes into account simple focal point connection and similarity across various cameras.
- Flexibility: C-Mount cameras are normally utilized in security frameworks, modern observing, and logical applications because of their versatility and adaptability.

PTZ camera

A PTZ (pan-tilt-zoom) camera is a sort of reconnaissance camera that can move evenly (skillet), in an upward direction (slant), and zoom in or out. It permits clients to remotely control the camera's development and change the zoom level, giving adaptable inclusion of various regions for observing or observation purposes.
PTZ Pan Tilt & Zoom Cameras.

Features

- Dish: PTZ cameras can move evenly (left and right) to cover a wide region.
- Slant: They can move upward (all over) to change the survey point.
- Zoom: PTZ cameras can change the focal point to zoom in or out, considering close-up or far off sees.
- Controller: Clients can remotely control the camera's

development and zoom level.

- Pre-set positions: These cameras can be set to explicit situations for simple route.
- Movement following: A PTZ cameras can follow moving items consequently.
- Adaptable inclusion: PTZ cameras offer flexible reconnaissance by covering various points and distances.
- Remote control for dynamic monitoring.
- Reduced need for multiple fixed cameras.

HD Camera

HD (Superior quality) cameras utilized in framework include catching clear and nitty gritty pictures or recordings. These cameras, outfitted with high-goal sensors, record visuals of designs, streets, or regions for checking and examination purposes. They help in evaluating the condition, upkeep, and security of framework like extensions, streets, structures, and that's just the beginning, giving significant visual information to examinations and dynamic cycle's points and distances.

Tools are

- DVR Unit
- Monitor
- Router
- Internet connection
- Camera
- Remote Client
- Remote Storage
- SMPS
- BNC & DC

IP Camera

IP cameras catch pictures or recordings, transform them into computerized data, send that information through an organization like the web, store it on a focal framework, and permit approved clients to access and screen the recording for security or the board purposes.

Tools are

- Network Video Recorder
- HDMI Local Display playback
- PoE
- HDD
- Internet connection
- IP Camera
- Web Client
- Mobile App

Chapter 2

Components & Tools

- Basic Components and their functions
- Tools Required
- Accessories

Components & Tools

In this section, we'll investigate the pieces that make up your CCTV framework and the devices you'll have to unite everything. Envision your CCTV framework as a riddle, and we're here to assist you with setting up the pieces. From cameras to links, we'll direct you through each move toward straight forward terms, ensuring you have the right devices to make it happen. In this way, we should begin on building a protected and careful focus around your space!

Any CCTV Specialized labourer to be required this part and Devices for better work .An electronic part is any fundamental discrete electronic gadget or actual substance some portion of an electronic framework used to influence electrons or their related fields.

Electronic parts have various electrical terminals or leads. These leads associate with other electrical parts, a device is an item that can stretch out a singular's capacity to change elements of the general climate or assist them with achieving a specific errand.

Basic components and their functions

BNC Connector for Video
Uses in

- Use in DVR/XVR Device
- 3+1 (Coaxial Cable)
- HD Camera

RJ 45 connector
Uses in

- **NVR Device**
- **Cat 6 cable**
- **IP Camera**

Video Balloon for CCTV
Uses in

- **DVR/NVR Device**
- **Cat 6 cable**
- **HD Camera**

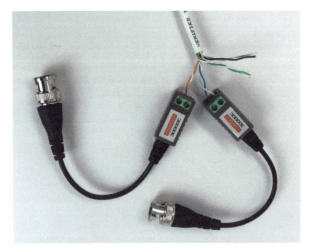

DC connector

A DC connector is a kind of electrical connector used to communicate direct flow (DC) power between electronic gadgets and power sources. They come in different shapes and sizes, offering a solid and normalized method for power association in electronic frameworks.

CCTV Twisted Pair Balloons

CCTV Contorted Pair Inflatable's are a minimized and productive answer for communicating video signals over significant distances utilizing curved pair links. These gadgets assist with limiting sign impedance and guarantee solid reconnaissance film transmission in CCTV frameworks.

<u>**Tools Required**</u>

Multi-meter

A computerized multi-meter is a test device used to gauge at least two electrical qualities — chiefly voltage (volts), flow (amps) and opposition (ohms). It is a standard symptomatic device for experts in the electrical/electronic businesses.

Audio connector

A sound connector in CCTV frameworks works with the transmission of sound signs close by video takes care of. Normally utilizing RCA or 3.5mm jacks, these connectors empower the coordination of amplifiers or speakers, improving reconnaissance abilities by catching and communicating sound.

Audio Pickup Microphone

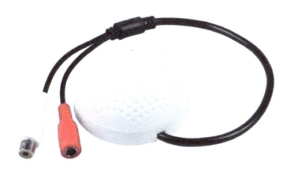

"3 +1 wire" configuration

In CCTV systems, the "3 +1 wire" configuration refers to a setup where video, power, and audio signals are transmitted through three separate wires. This arrangement simplifies installation and maintenance processes, allowing for efficient connectivity and organization of cables. It ensures reliable and clear transmission of multimedia data for surveillance purposes.

- Yellow - Audio
- Red- Positive +
- Black- Native –

Power Supply

The power supply of a CCTV framework is crucial for steady

activity, giving power to cameras, recorders, and peripherals. Commonly, it changes over AC mains capacity to DC, offering stable voltage levels. A solid power supply guarantees continuous observation, shields against power floods, and supports the usefulness of the whole CCTV organization.

Type of Power Supply

Centralized
Utilizes a single power source for multiple cameras, simplifying installation and management.

Distributed
Employs individual power adapters for each camera, offering flexibility but requiring more wiring.

SMPS

Switched Mode Power Supply (SMPS) is a typical power hotspot for CCTV frameworks. It proficiently changes over AC capacity to managed DC, offering stable voltage levels for cameras and different parts. SMPS units are reduced, lightweight, and give dependable power, guaranteeing continuous reconnaissance activities in different conditions.

POE Camera Data & Power Solution

POE (Power over Ethernet) Camera Information and Power Arrangement is a cutting edge development in CCTV innovation. It coordinates the two information transmission and power supply over a solitary Ethernet link, working on establishment and diminishing link mess. POE cameras wipe out the requirement for discrete power sources, improving adaptability and cost-viability in reconnaissance arrangements.

The concept is straightforward. When you see the camera's RJ45 socket, connect a Cat6 punch-down cable to the camera port and the PoE RJ45 socket. Then, connect the uplink to the NVR.

Monitor Mounts

A screen mount, otherwise called a screen arm or screen section, is a gadget that holds up a PC screen, PC, or other showcase screen. Screen mounts are normally clipped to the rear of a wall area.

Rack

A rack in CCTV is a design that holds DVR or PC servers or systems administration hardware. Racks are commonly comprised of vertical segments and level retires that structure an edge. They are frequently encased to guarantee security.

Mouse

A remote mouse can be utilized with CCTV framework 2 DVR recorders. The mouse accompanies batteries and a little recipient that plugs into the DVR recorder..

Wifi Dongle

A WiFi dongle is a pivotal part in CCTV frameworks. It works with remote availability, empowering cameras to associate with the web for remote observing. This little gadget connects to a camera's opening and lays out an association with the WiFi organization of the framework. WiFi dongles improve the adaptability and simplicity of arrangement in CCTV frameworks, assuming an essential part in CCTV innovation.

Wifi router

A WiFi Router is essential to CCTV arrangements, giving remote network to cameras. It fills in as a focal center point, empowering the cameras to interface with the web. This availability takes into account remote checking and the board of the CCTV framework. WiFi switches upgrade the adaptability of camera situation and add to the productivity of observation frameworks by empowering consistent information transmission and access.

Hammer

In CCTV contexts, the hammer serves as a symbol of protection and deterrence against vandalism and intrusion. It represents the proactive measures necessary to secure premises and assets, emphasizing the importance of robust surveillance systems for safety and security.

Pliers

Pliers in CCTV symbolize precision and fine-tuning. They represent the meticulous adjustments and maintenance required for optimal camera positioning and functionality. Like pliers, attention to detail ensures effective surveillance, enhancing security and monitoring capabilities.

Wire cutter

In the realm of CCTV, wire cutters serve as tools of adaptation and customization. They signify the ability to tailor wiring installations for optimal camera placement and connectivity. Wire cutters ensure efficient cable management, enabling seamless integration and reliable surveillance functionality.

LAN Tester

A LAN tester is an essential tool in CCTV installations, ensuring the integrity and functionality of network connections. It verifies Ethernet cables, identifies wiring faults, and validates network configurations. By pinpointing issues promptly, LAN testers facilitate efficient troubleshooting and maintenance, guaranteeing reliable data transmission and optimal performance in CCTV systems .

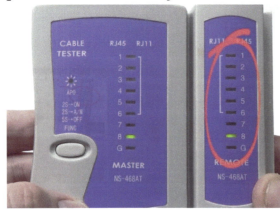

LAN crimping tool

A LAN crimping tool is indispensable in CCTV installations for terminating Ethernet cables with RJ45 connectors. It allows technicians to create custom-length cables tailored to specific camera placements and networking requirements. This tool ensures reliable connections, minimizes signal interference, and enhances the efficiency and flexibility of CCTV network setups.

Screwdriver

In CCTV installations, a screwdriver symbolizes precision and stability. It is vital for securely fastening cameras, mounts, and other components. Like a screwdriver, attention to detail ensures stable installations, guaranteeing effective surveillance and optimal security coverage.

Drill bit

When installing a CCTV camera, you can use a drill bit that is the same size as the screws that came with the camera. You can use the mounting template that comes with most camera kits as a guide to place the screws correctly.

Drill machines

Drill machines in CCTV installations bolster security by deterring vandalism and unauthorized tampering. Their strategic placement ensures robust mounting of cameras and equipment, safeguarding against theft and manipulation. This integration enhances surveillance integrity, fortifying critical areas effectively.

12v 1A power supply

A 12V 1A power supply in CCTV systems delivers stable electricity to cameras, ensuring uninterrupted surveillance operations. With its low voltage and adequate current output, it's compatible with most CCTV devices. This power source enhances system reliability, enabling continuous monitoring and reliable security coverage.

Measuring Tape

Measuring tape in CCTV setups aids in precise camera placement and field of view calculation. It ensures optimal coverage and accurate distance measurements between cameras and objects of interest. This tool facilitates efficient installation, calibration, and maintenance of surveillance systems, enhancing overall security effectiveness.

Cleaning Brush

A cleaning brush is essential in CCTV maintenance for removing dust, dirt, and debris that accumulate on camera lenses and housings. Regular cleaning ensures clear and unobstructed views, maximizing image quality and system performance. This simple tool extends the lifespan of CCTV equipment and enhances overall surveillance effectiveness.

Tool Bag

A CCTV tool bag is a portable kit containing essential equipment for installing, maintaining, and troubleshooting surveillance systems. It typically includes items like screwdrivers, pliers, cable testers, connectors, and other specialized tools. The bag ensures technicians have everything they need on hand for efficient CCTV work, improving productivity and service quality.

Wire Cutter

Wire cutters are indispensable tools in CCTV installations, allowing technicians to trim and strip cables with precision. They ensure neat and secure connections between cameras, DVRs, and power sources, minimizing signal loss and potential hazards. Wire cutters facilitate efficient wiring, contributing to reliable and effective surveillance system deployment.

Black Tape for Wire Cover

Black tape for wire cover is a versatile accessory in CCTV installations, used to conceal and protect exposed wires. Its adhesive properties secure wires in place, preventing tripping hazards and maintaining a neat appearance. This simple yet effective solution enhances safety and aesthetics in surveillance setups.

Accessories

The embellishments in a CCTV system include various essential components such as mounting brackets, junction boxes, cables, and connectors. These accessories facilitate installation, improve camera positioning, and ensure proper cable management. They play a crucial role in enhancing the functionality and effectiveness of surveillance systems, offering versatility and reliability.

Useful Accessories for Betterment

WIRELESS MOUSE

WI-FI DONGLE

POE BOX

Storage Friendly design

 Solid Metal Welded

Screw included in the box

Chapter 3

CCTV Infrastructure System Design

- ◦ Camera selection and placement
- ◦ Lens selection and field of view

◦ **Monitor & Rack Selection**

Introduction:

In summary, the CCTV System Model Documents will provide documentation templates that will guide the user through the selection and insertion of applicable user needs, . The Model Documents will provide guidance to the user on selecting operational CCTV system capabilities that fit within the use cases and operational scenarios. The focus of this guidance a CCTV system that is currently available in the product market.

What is a Site Survey ?

A site survey in CCTV design involves a comprehensive assessment of the location where the surveillance system will be installed. It includes examining the physical layout, identifying key areas that require monitoring, assessing lighting conditions, and evaluating potential obstacles or challenges. The site survey helps determine the optimal placement of cameras, the type of cameras needed, and the infrastructure requirements for effective surveillance coverage. It ensures that the CCTV system is tailored to the specific needs and characteristics of the site, maximizing its effectiveness in enhancing security and surveillance.

Understanding the Landscape :

Understanding the landscape is a critical aspect of the CCTV installation process. It involves gaining insight into the physical environment where the surveillance system will operate. Factors such as terrain, lighting conditions, architectural features, and potential obstructions must be considered. This understanding enables technicians to make informed decisions regarding camera placement, cabling routes, and overall system design, ensuring optimal coverage and effectiveness in monitoring the area.

The Importance of Site Assessment :

The importance of site assessment in CCTV installation cannot be overstated. It serves as the foundation for designing an effective surveillance system tailored to the specific needs and characteristics of the location. Site assessment involves analysing the layout, identifying critical areas for monitoring, evaluating lighting conditions, and recognizing potential challenges or vulnerabilities.

By conducting a thorough site assessment, technicians can determine the optimal placement of cameras, select appropriate equipment, and plan the infrastructure required for seamless integration. This process ensures that the CCTV system provides comprehensive coverage, minimizes blind spots, and addresses security concerns effectively.

Moreover, site assessment enables the identification of potential risks and vulnerabilities, allowing for the implementation of proactive security measures. It helps in developing strategies to mitigate threats and enhance overall security posture.

In essence, site assessment is a fundamental step in the CCTV installation process, providing valuable insights that shape the design, functionality, and performance of the surveillance system. It lays the groundwork for a robust security infrastructure that helps safeguard assets, deter criminal activity, and maintain a safe environment.

Steps in Site Survey for CCTV Installation

- Preparation: Gather necessary tools and equipment for the survey, including measuring tape, camera placement diagrams, and a notebook for documentation.
- Review Site Plans: Obtain blueprints or site plans to understand the layout, entrances, exits, and potential areas of interest.
- Walkthrough: Conduct a physical walkthrough of the

site to familiarize yourself with the terrain, existing structures, and any potential obstacles.

- **Identify Key Areas:** Determine critical areas that require surveillance coverage, such as entry points, parking lots, corridors, and high-value assets.
- **Assess Lighting Conditions:** Evaluate natural and artificial lighting conditions throughout the day to identify areas with poor visibility or excessive glare.
- **Check for Obstructions:** Note any obstructions like trees, buildings, or signage that may block camera views or impede signal transmission.
- **Measure Distances:** Use a measuring tape to determine the distance between camera locations, control rooms, and power sources for accurate cabling and power supply planning.
- **Consider Environmental Factors:** Take into account environmental factors such as weather conditions, temperature variations, and exposure to dust or moisture.
- **Review Security Requirements:** Understand specific security requirements and compliance standards relevant to the site, including data protection regulations and privacy laws.
- **Document Findings:** Record detailed observations, measurements, and any site-specific considerations in a comprehensive report or survey document.
- **Consult with Stakeholders:** Communicate findings and recommendations with relevant stakeholders, including property owners, security personnel, and project managers.
- **Finalize Design Proposal:** Based on the site survey findings, develop a customized CCTV system design proposal that addresses security needs, budget constraints, and technical requirements.

Camera Selection:

- **Resolution:** Choose cameras with appropriate resolution levels based on the required image clarity and detail. Higher resolution cameras provide clearer images but may require more storage space.
- **Lens Type:** Select lenses based on the desired field of view. Varifocal lenses offer adjustable focal lengths for flexibility in capturing wide-angle or narrow views.
- **Weatherproof Ratings:** Opt for cameras with weatherproof ratings suitable for outdoor installation, ensuring durability and longevity in harsh environmental conditions.
- **Night Vision:** Consider cameras with infrared (IR) or low-light capabilities for clear surveillance footage in low-light or nighttime conditions.
- **Pan-Tilt-Zoom (PTZ) Functionality:** PTZ cameras allow remote control of pan, tilt, and zoom functions, providing flexibility in monitoring and tracking moving objects or subjects.
- **Wide Dynamic Range (WDR):** Cameras with WDR technology capture clear images in high-contrast lighting conditions, reducing overexposure or underexposure in challenging environments.
- **Audio and Two-Way Communication:** Cameras with built-in microphones or support for two-way communication enable audio monitoring and interaction, enhancing situational awareness and security response capabilities.
- **Integration Compatibility:** Ensure cameras are compatible with the chosen DVR/NVR system and support integration with other security devices or software platforms for seamless operation.

Deference Between

HD Camera (High Definition)	IP Camera (Internet Protocol)
Good Picture Quality	Better Picture Quality like Smartphone Camera
Durability 3-5 Year +	Durability 5 - 8 Year +
Yearly Basis Maintenance Required	Low Maintenance
Normal Affordable Price	Expensive
No Identification internet	Own IP for Identification internet
No Software	Advanced Software Support
Etc	Etc

Camera Placement

- **Identify Critical Areas:** Determine key areas requiring surveillance coverage, such as entry points, parking lots, corridors, and high-value assets.
- **Field of View:** Position cameras to achieve optimal coverage of the target area while minimizing blind spots and ensuring overlap for comprehensive surveillance.
- **Height and Angle:** Mount cameras at an appropriate height and angle to capture clear and unobstructed views of the monitored area. Avoid placing cameras too high or too low, which may compromise image quality and coverage.
- **Strategic Placement:** Place cameras strategically to

deter criminal activity, monitor access points, and provide visibility of vulnerable areas.

- Consider Lighting Conditions: Take into account natural and artificial lighting conditions to avoid glare, shadows, or overexposure that may affect camera performance and image quality.
- Secure Mounting: Ensure cameras are securely mounted to prevent tampering or vandalism. Use sturdy mounting brackets and consider anti-vandalism features for added protection.
- Cabling and Power Supply: Plan cabling routes and ensure sufficient power supply for cameras, taking into consideration distance limitations and voltage requirements.
- Regulatory Compliance: Adhere to legal and regulatory requirements regarding camera placement, data privacy, and surveillance signage to maintain compliance and mitigate legal risks.

Lens selection and field of view are critical components of the CCTV installation process, impacting the surveillance system's effectiveness in monitoring and capturing relevant footage.

Lens Selection

- Focal Length: The focal length of a lens determines its angle of view and magnification. Shorter focal lengths provide a wider field of view, while longer focal lengths offer greater magnification and narrower fields of view.
- Fixed vs. Varifocal Lenses: Fixed lenses have a static focal length, providing a consistent field of view. Varifocal lenses offer adjustable focal lengths, allowing for flexibility in adjusting the field of view as needed.
- Aperture: The aperture of a lens controls the amount of light entering the camera. Larger aperture sizes allow more light to pass through, making them suitable for low-light conditions.

- Lens Quality: High-quality lenses with advanced coatings and optical elements minimize distortion, aberrations, and image degradation, ensuring clear and sharp footage.
- Compatibility: Ensure compatibility between the lens and the camera model to optimize performance and image quality.

Field of View (FOV):
- Determining Coverage Area: The field of view refers to the area visible to the camera lens. It is determined by the lens focal length and camera placement.
- Calculating FOV: The FOV can be calculated based on the camera's focal length, sensor size, and distance from the target area. Various online calculators and software tools are available to assist in calculating FOV.
- Considerations for FOV: Consider factors such as the desired level of detail, the distance to the subject, and the width of the area to be monitored when determining the FOV.
- Overlap and Blind Spots: Ensure sufficient overlap between camera coverage areas to minimize blind spots and ensure comprehensive surveillance coverage.
- Adjustability: Varifocal lenses offer the flexibility to adjust the FOV by changing the focal length, allowing for fine-tuning of the surveillance area based on specific requirements.
- Optimizing FOV: Optimize the FOV to capture critical areas of interest while avoiding unnecessary coverage of irrelevant spaces, maximizing the effectiveness and efficiency of the surveillance system.

Monitor Selection

If Your Machine Setup in Desk then you can use normal lcd it's ok , But your monitor hang in wall then
You have to use Led display otherwise , camera footage not understand clear your client will be unhappy.
So recommend use led display , also if you are using higher channel Machine then must be used big display size ,
Like 18.5, 22, 24, 32 inch for Better View.

Rack Selection

Rack is Protector of Your Machine form Teaf , So , if Possible use rack in wall hanging all machine for safe Everything .

Generally rack is Available 2U, 4U, 8U you used always 4U for better work Space & air Flow for not Hitting Device & cool.

Chapter 4

Machine, Hard Disk & Cable Selection

- ∘ Machine
- ∘ Hard Disk
- ∘ Cable Selection

- · Machine Means DVR/NVR/XVR

Machine and cable selection are pivotal steps in the CCTV installation process, ensuring the reliable operation and connectivity of the surveillance system.

Machine Selection

- DVR/NVR: Choose a Digital Video Recorder (DVR) or Network Video Recorder (NVR) based on the specific requirements of the surveillance system. Consider factors such as the number of camera channels, storage capacity, resolution support, and remote access capabilities.
- Quality and Reliability: Select machines from reputable manufacturers known for producing high-quality, reliable surveillance equipment. Ensure compatibility with the chosen cameras and other system components.
- Remote Access Features: DVR/NVR models that offer remote access capabilities, allowing users to view live footage and playback recordings from any internet-enabled device.
- Scalability: Consider the scalability of the DVR/NVR system to accommodate future expansion or additional camera installations as surveillance needs evolve.
- Power Supply: Ensure the DVR/NVR has a reliable power supply with adequate surge protection to prevent damage from power fluctuations or electrical surges.

Hard disk

This is a storage device which is used for storing the captured video with the use of a security camera to have it used later. These devices can be fitted within the video recorders and can be viewed by connecting to the DVR monitor directly.

SSD

A solid-state drive is a solid-state storage device that uses integrated circuit assemblies to store data persistently, typically using flash memory, and functions as secondary storage in the hierarchy of computer storage, if Possible use it for Better Life Camera Data.

Type of Cables

Coaxial cable

Coaxial cable is a versatile electrical cable used for transmitting high-frequency signals like video and data. Its construction includes a central conductor, insulating layer, metallic shield, and outer insulating layer. Coaxial cables offer efficient signal transmission with minimal interference, making them ideal for CCTV systems.

Cat 6 (Normally Used for Internet)

Cat6, or Category 6, is a type of twisted pair cable commonly used for internet connections. It offers higher bandwidth and faster data transmission compared to previous versions like Cat5. Cat6 cables have stringent specifications for reducing crosstalk and interference, making them suitable for demanding networking applications. They are often utilized in home and office networks, providing reliable and high-speed internet connectivity.

Cable Selection:

- Type of Cable: Select the appropriate type of cable for data and power transmission based on the specific requirements of the CCTV system. Common cable types include coaxial cables, Ethernet cables (Cat5e or Cat6), and power cables.
- Quality and Durability: Choose cables made from high-quality materials with proper shielding to minimize signal interference, ensure data integrity, and maintain reliable connectivity.
- Length and Gauge: Determine the required cable length and gauge based on the distance between cameras, DVR/NVR, and power sources. Use thicker gauge cables

for longer distances to minimize voltage drop and signal degradation.

· **Weatherproofing:** For outdoor installations, use weatherproof cables designed to with stand exposure to harsh environmental conditions such as moisture, UV radiation, and temperature extremes. If Possible use PVC Casing for long life Cable.

· **Connector Compatibility:** Ensure compatibility between the cables and connectors used in the CCTV system to facilitate easy installation and reliable connections.

· **Cable Management:** Plan and organize cable routes to minimize clutter, prevent tangling, and maintain a neat and professional installation appearance. Use cable management accessories such as conduit, raceways, and cable ties as needed.

· **Testing and Certification:** Test cables for continuity, signal integrity, and proper installation before finalizing the CCTV system setup. Ensure compliance with industry standards and regulations for cable installation and certification.

Chapter 5

Installation and Configuration
  ◦ **Mounting and Positioning cameras**

- ○ Cable routing and Power supply installation (SMPS or PoE)
- ○ DVR/NVR/XVR setup and configuration

Mounting and positioning cameras

Introduction

CCTV cameras help us keep places safe by watching them all the time. In this chapter, we will learn how to mount (fix) and position (place) these cameras in the right spots.

Tools You Will Need :

Before we start, gather these tools:

- A screwdriver
- Screws
- A drill
- Mounting brackets (holders for the camera)
- A ladder (if needed)
- Measuring tape

Choosing the Right Spot

- Where you put your camera is very important. Follow these steps to find the best spot:
- High Up: Place the camera high enough so people cannot reach it easily. This also gives a better view.
- Good View: Choose a spot that covers the main areas you want to watch, like doors, windows, or driveways.
- Lighting: Make sure the camera is not directly facing a bright light, like the sun or a lamp, as it can make the picture unclear.
- The coverage area of a camera always depends on its resolution. It's important to understand the clear distinction from the start of the coverage area to the end.
- For instance, if a company claims a camera covers 70

feet, it actually provides a better view up to 50 feet. Additionally, there is always a gap of 4 to 6 feet from the camera placement to the start of the viewing point which is not covered.

· This is because cameras are machines, not human beings. Humans can see 360 degrees, but a camera can only see or watch 180 degrees at a time within a specified angle, which results in different coverage outcomes.

Mounting the Camera

· 1. Mark the Spot: Use the mounting bracket to mark where you will drill holes on the wall.
· 2. Drill Holes: Carefully drill holes where you marked.
· 3. Fix the Bracket: Use screws to fix the mounting bracket to the wall.
· 4. Attach the Camera: Place the camera on the bracket and secure it with screws.

Positioning the Camera

· Adjust the Angle: Tilt and turn the camera to get the best view of the area. Make sure it covers all important spots.
· Test the View: Check the camera feed on your monitor or phone to see if the view is clear and covers the desired area.
· Tighten Screws: Once the angle is perfect, tighten all screws to keep the camera steady.

Connecting the Camera

· Wired Cameras: Connect the camera to the power supply and the DVR (Digital Video Recorder) using cables.
· Wireless Cameras: Connect the camera to the power supply and follow the instructions to connect it to your Wi-Fi.

Final Checks

- **Clear View:** Ensure there are no obstacles blocking the camera's view.
- **Stable Mounting:** Make sure the camera is firmly attached and does not move.
- **Good Connection:** Check the camera feed again to ensure everything is working properly.

Maintenance Tips

- **Regular Cleaning:** Wipe the camera lens regularly to keep the view clear.
- **Check Mounting:** Occasionally check the screws and brackets to make sure they are still tight.
- **Update Software:** If your camera uses software, keep it updated for the best performance

Cable Routing and Termination

Introduction

When setting up a CCTV system, one of the most important tasks is to correctly route and terminate the cables. This means you need to carefully place the cables from the cameras to the recording device and make sure they are connected properly. Let's break down the steps to make it simple.

What You Need

- CCTV cameras

- Cables (usually coaxial or Ethernet)

- Cable ties

- Drill (if needed)

- Screwdrivers

- Cable connectors (like BNC connectors for coaxial cables or RJ45 connectors for Ethernet cables)

- Cable tester (optional but helpful)

Step-by-Step Guide

Planning Your Cable Route

Before you start, decide where your cameras and recording device (DVR or NVR) will be located. Then, plan the path the cables will take to connect them. Consider the following:

- Avoid high traffic areas where people might trip over the cables.

- Try to keep the cables away from power lines to avoid interference.

- Plan to route cables through walls, ceilings, or conduits if necessary for protection.

Measuring and Cutting Cables

Measure the distance from each camera to the recording device. Add a few extra feet to each measurement to ensure you have enough cable. Cut the cables to the appropriate lengths using wire cutters.

Drilling Holes (if necessary)

If you need to run cables through walls or ceilings, use a drill to make holes. Be sure to check for any hidden wires or pipes before drilling. It's a good idea to use a stud finder to avoid hitting structural supports.

Routing the Cables

Carefully feed the cables through the drilled holes or conduits. Use cable ties to secure the cables along their route, making sure they are neatly organized and not dangling.

Connecting the Cables

Each type of cable has a specific connector. Here's how to attach the connectors:

For Coaxial Cables (BNC Connector):

1. Strip about 1 inch of the outer insulation of the cable.

2. Peel back the shielding and strip about 1/4 inch of the inner insulation to expose the copper wire.

3. Slide the BNC connector parts onto the cable.

4. Crimp the connector onto the cable using a crimping tool.

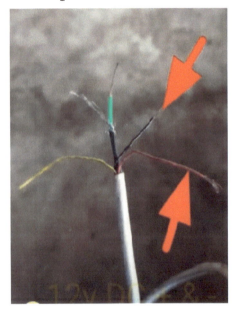

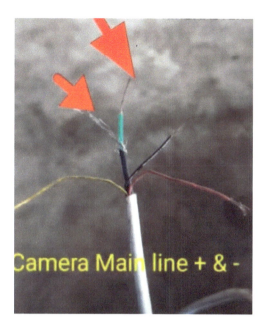

Camera Main line + & -

For Ethernet Cables or Cat6 (RJ45 Connector):

1. Strip about 1 inch of the outer insulation of the cable.

2. Untwist the wire pairs and arrange them in the correct order (there are two standards: T568A and T568B).

3. Trim the wires evenly, about 1/2 inch long.

4. Insert the wires into the RJ45 connector, making sure each wire is in the correct slot.

5. Crimp the connector onto the cable using a crimping tool.

RJ45 Pinout
T-568B

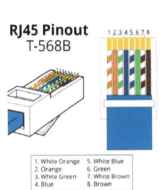

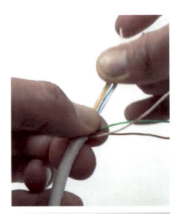

1. White Orange
2. Orange
3. White Green
4. Blue
5. White Blue
6. Green
7. White Brown
8. Brown

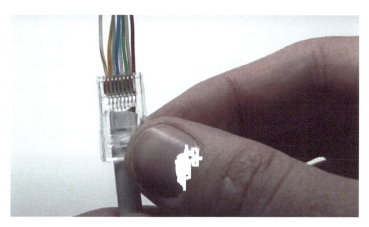

Testing the Connections

Use a Lan cable tester to check if the cables are properly connected. This tool will help you identify any connection problems. Plug one end of the cable into the tester and the other end into the corresponding device (camera or recording device). If the tester shows a good connection, you're ready to go.

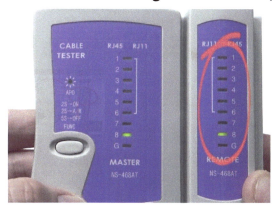

Connecting to the Devices

Finally, plug the cables into your CCTV cameras and the recording device. Make sure each camera is connected to the correct input on the recorder. Power on the system and check if the cameras are displaying video correctly.

Troubleshooting Tips

No Video Signal: Check the cable connections and ensure the connectors are properly attached. Test the cable with a tester.

Interference: Ensure the cables are not running too close to power lines or other electrical devices.

Loose Connections: Make sure all connectors are tightly crimped and securely plugged into the devices.

Conclusion

Routing and terminating cables might seem tricky at first, but by following these steps carefully, you can set up your CCTV system correctly. Take your time, double-check your connections, and soon you'll have a fully functioning security system.

Power Supply Installation

Introduction

Welcome to the Subject on power supply installation for your CCTV system! This guide will help you understand how to provide power to your cameras in an easy and safe way. Let's get started!

What is a Power Supply?

A power supply is a device that gives your CCTV cameras the

electricity they need to work. Think of it like a battery for a toy. Without power, your cameras won't be able to see anything.

Types of Power Supplies

Plug-in Adapter: This is like the charger for your phone. You plug it into the wall socket, and it powers your camera.

Power over Ethernet (PoE):This type uses the same cable for both power and data. It's like getting internet and electricity from the same wire!

Tools You Will Need

- **Power Supply (Adapter or PoE)**
- **CCTV Camera**
- **Power Cables**
- **Screwdriver**
- **Electrical Tape**

Steps to Install a Power Supply

Choose a Location for the Power Supply

 - Find a place near your camera where you can easily connect the power supply.

  - Make sure it's a dry and safe spot to avoid any electrical hazards.

Connect the Power Adapter (for Plug-in Adapter)

- Take the plug-in adapter and insert it into the wall socket.

- Connect the other end to your CCTV camera. Look for a round port on the camera marked "DC" or "Power."

Using PoE (Power over Ethernet)

- IP camera supports PoE, use an Ethernet cable. This cable looks like a thick phone wire.

- Plug one end of the Ethernet cable into the camera and the other end into a PoE switch or injector.

Secure the Connections

- Make sure all the plugs are firmly connected. Loose connections can cause your camera to lose power.

- Use electrical tape to cover any exposed wires to prevent accidents.

Test the Camera

- Turn on the power supply.

- Check if the camera is working. You should see lights on the camera indicating its getting power.

Safety Tips

Turn Off the Power before Working

- Always make sure the power is off before connecting or disconnecting anything.

Avoid Water

- Never install the power supply where it can get wet. Water and electricity are dangerous together.

Check for Damage

- Inspect all cables and the power supply for any signs of damage before use. Damaged wires can cause fires.

Troubleshooting

Camera Not Turning On: Check if the power supply is properly plugged in. Ensure the socket has power by testing it with another device.

Flickering Camera: This could be due to a loose connection. Recheck all plugs and secure them tightly.
Overheating: If the power supply feels too hot, turn it off and let it cool. Make sure it's in a well-ventilated area.

Summary

Installing a power supply for your CCTV camera is like giving it food. It's essential for its operation. By following these simple steps and safety tips, you can ensure your camera is powered up and ready to protect your home or business.
Remember, always be careful when working with electricity and if you're unsure, ask for help from someone who knows about electrical work.

Introduction to DVR/NVR/XVR

DVR (Digital Video Recorder):A device that records video from analog cameras. It saves videos on a hard drive and allows you to play them back later.

NVR (Network Video Recorder): A device that records video from digital (IP) cameras. It also saves videos on a hard drive and allows for playback.

XVR (Hybrid Video Recorder):A device that can work with both analog and IP cameras. It combines features of both DVR and NVR.

Getting Started

Unboxing and Checking

Open the box: Carefully remove the DVR/NVR/XVR from the box.

Check the contents: Ensure you have the DVR/NVR/XVR, power adapter, Mouse, user manual, and any other accessories like Cables.

Setting Up the Device

Choose a Location: Place your DVR/NVR/XVR in a cool, dry place. Avoid direct sunlight and ensure it has proper ventilation.

Connect to Power: Plug the power adapter into the DVR/NVR/XVR and then into a wall outlet.

Connect to Monitor: Use an HDMI or VGA cable to connect the DVR/NVR/XVR to a monitor or TV. This allows you to Display Output the camera feeds and configure the device.

Connecting Cameras

Analog Cameras (for DVR/XVR)

Connect Camera to DVR/XVR : Use a coaxial cable to connect the camera to one of the video input ports on the DVR/XVR Back Side Ports via BNC Connecter .

Power the Camera: Connect the camera to a power source using the power adapter(SMPS) provided With proper wiring Raping DC + - ,

IP Cameras (for NVR/XVR)

Connect Camera to NVR/XVR: Use an Ethernet cable to connect the camera to one of the network ports on the NVR/XVR.

Power the Camera: If the camera supports Power over Ethernet (PoE), it will receive power through the Ethernet cable. Otherwise, connect the camera to a power source.

Initial Configuration

Turning On the Device

Power On: Press the power button on the DVR/NVR/XVR. The device will start up and display a welcome screen on the monitor.

Setting Up the Device

Language Selection: Choose your preferred language for the system.

Date and Time: Set the correct date and time. This is important for accurate recording and playback.

Password: Create a strong password for the device. This will protect your system from unauthorized access.

Adding and Configuring Cameras

Adding Cameras

Automatic Search (for NVR/XVR): Go to the camera management section and click on "Add Camera" or "Search". The device will automatically detect connected IP cameras.

Manual Add (for DVR/XVR): For analog cameras, the device will automatically recognize the cameras once connected. You may need to assign each camera to a specific channel.

Camera Settings

Resolution: Choose the resolution for each camera. Higher resolution provides better image quality but uses more storage space.

Recording Mode: Select the recording mode:

Continuous: Records all the time.

Motion Detection: Records only when movement is detected.

Schedule: Records at specific times of the day.

Adjust Camera View: Use the on-screen controls to pan, tilt, and zoom the camera (if supported).

Setting Up Recording

Storage: Insert a hard drive into the DVR/NVR/XVR if not already installed. Follow the user manual for instructions on how to install it.

Recording Settings: Go to the recording settings and choose the storage location, recording mode, and video quality.

Playback

Access Playback: Go to the playback section on the DVR/NVR/XVR.

Select Date and Time: Choose the date and time range you want to view.

Play Video: Select the camera and click play to view recorded footage. Use the on-screen controls to pause, fast forward, or rewind.

Maintenance and Troubleshooting

Regular Maintenance

Check Connections: Regularly check all cables and connections to ensure they are secure.

Clean Cameras: Clean camera lenses with a soft, dry cloth to ensure clear images.

Update Firmware: Check for firmware updates for your DVR/NVR/XVR and apply them to ensure optimal performance and security.

Conclusion

You have now set up and configured your DVR/NVR/XVR system. With regular maintenance and proper configuration, your CCTV system will provide reliable security and surveillance. If you have any issues, refer to this manual or contact customer support for assistance.

This simple guide covers the basics of setting up and configuring a DVR, NVR, or XVR system. It is designed to be easy to understand.

Chapter 6

Video Analytics and Advanced Features
- Introduction to video analytics
- Motion detection and object tracking
- Video Export for as per Required /Backup

Video Analytics and Advanced Features

CLICK MAIN MENU -> PLAYBACK

SELECT DATE & CAMERA NUMBER SELECT

SIMPLE CLICK NOW PLAY ICON & IF YOU WANT TO CHANGE TIME THEN YOU CAN USE BAR SECTION.

Motion detection and object tracking

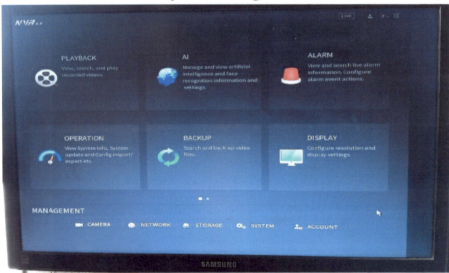

CLICK MAIN MENU AFTER YOU WILL GET SEE ALL MENU THEN YOU SELECT AI , OPEN MENU & SET PARAMETER IT'S DEPENDING ON CAMERA MODEL FUNCTION SUPPORT & RESTART SYSTEM AFTER WORKING AI FUNCTION.

Video Export for as per Required /Backup

CLIENT MAIN MENU AFTER YOU WILL GET SEE BACKUP, BEFORE CLICK YOU HAVE MUST BE ALREADY PLUG-IN PEN DRIVE INTO VIA USB SOCKET. THEN CLICK BACKUP MENU.

NOW YOU WILL SEE BACKUP MENU OPTION ,SETUP :- SELECT PEN DRIVE ,SELECT CAMERA NUMBER THEN SELECT DATE & FILE FORMAT WHICH YOU WANT . LAST ONE START TIME

PROPER & END TIME PROPER THEN YOU GET VIDEO LIST , FINALLY YOU CLICK BACKUP THEN FILE WILL BE COPY YOUR PEN DRIVE , IT'S TAKE SOME TIME DEPENDING ON FILE SIZE ALSO SHOW PROGRESS BAR , AFTER COMPLETE HOLE FILE COPY YOUR PEN DRIVE THEN UN-PLUG PEN DRIVE .

Network & Mobile View Configuration
- **What is Network & IP**
- **Network configuration and remote access**
- **Mobile Application Download & Setup View Camera**

Network and Mobile View Configuration

Network :

A computer network is a system that connects two or more computing devices for transmitting and sharing information. Computing devices include everything from a mobile phone to a server. These devices are connected using physical wires such as fiber optics, but they can also be wireless.

Two very common types of networks include:

- Local Area Network (LAN)
- Wide Area Network (WAN)

IP Address

An IP address is a string of numbers separated by periods. IP addresses are expressed as a set of four numbers — an example address might be 192.158.1.38. Each number in the set can range from 0 to 255. So, the full IP addressing range goes from 0.0.0.0 to 255.255.255.255.

IP addresses are not random. They are mathematically produced and allocated by the Internet Assigned Numbers Authority (IANA), a division of the Internet Corporation for Assigned Names and Numbers (ICANN). ICANN is a non-profit organization that was established in the United States in 1998 to help maintain the security of the internet and allow it to be usable by all. Each time anyone registers a domain on the internet, they go through a domain name registrar, who pays a small fee to ICANN to register the domain.

Network configuration and remote access

Introduction

Welcome! In this chapter, we will learn about how to set up your CCTV system so you can view it from anywhere, using the internet. This is called "network configuration and remote access." Don't worry, we'll keep it simple!

What is Network Configuration?

Network configuration is like setting up a map that tells your CCTV camera how to connect to your home or business internet. This allows your camera to send video footage to your computer or phone.

Network Configuration

Connecting to the Internet

Wired Connection: Connect an Ethernet cable from the DVR/NVR/XVR to your router & Go To network Section

Select DSHP Mode its Easy work for normally after restart if router have internet automatic device online.

Wireless Connection: If the device supports Wi-Fi, go to network settings and select your Wi-Fi network. Enter the Wi-Fi password to connect. Select DSHP Mode its Easy work for normally after restart if router have internet automatic device online.

CLIENT MAIN MENU AFTER YOU WILL GET SEE NETWORK, THEN YOU CLICK EDIT OPTION GET POP-UP WINDOW ,THEN SIMPLE CLICK DHCP MODE AND RESTART SYSTEM . AFTER GET DEVICE ONLINE IF ROUTER HAVE INTERNET.

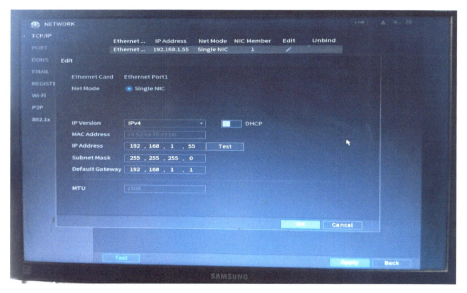

Remote Access / P2P

Enable Remote Access: Go to network settings and enable remote access. This allows you to view the camera feeds from your smartphone or computer.

Set Up DDNS (Optional): If your internet service provider uses a dynamic IP address, set up Dynamic DNS (DDNS) to ensure you can always access your system remotely.

Step-by-Step Guide to Network Configuration

Connect Your CCTV to the Router:

- Your CCTV camera needs to be connected to the internet. Use an Ethernet cable to connect your CCTV camera to your router. The router is the device that connects all your home devices to the internet.

What is Remote Access?

Remote access allows you to view your CCTV camera from anywhere in the world, using your smartphone, tablet, or computer. You just need an internet connection.

Access Your CCTV from a Smartphone:

- Download a CCTV app on your smartphone. Many CCTV camera manufacturers have their own apps.

- Open the app and enter your DDNS address (e.g., `mycamera.ddns.net`) and the port number (e.g., `8080`).

Enter your camera's username and password. Now you can view your CCTV camera from your smartphone!

Chapter 8

Live Project Hand on Practices
- ◦ **Wi-Fi Camera Setup**
- ◦ **HD Camera Setup**
- ◦ **IP Camera Setup**

- • **Live Project Hand on Practices**

- **Wi-Fi Camera Setup**
- **Download Application from App Store & Open, Now You See Create Account.**

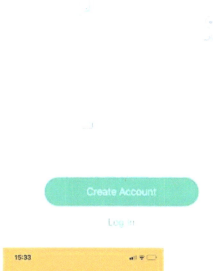

Create Account

Log in

Power on Camera

Plug in the device. Wait until you hear "Ready to pair".

I heard "Ready to pair"

Didn't hear "Ready to pair"?

Prepare another device as your camera

Select your device type

Mobile Device
Download the Alfred app on another Android/iOS device

AlfredCam
Set up the Alfred-made hardware camera

Computer
Open Alfred's WebCamera on your browser

Scan the QR code using your camera

This code will expire in 30 min 00 sec.

I heard QR code Scanned

Not sure how to scan?

HD Camera Setup

Flow the Diagram & Connect Wire each other device as per previews guide chapters and plug-in electric socket for supply power on , if you every connation properly good within 2 Minute All Camera will be Live Show on your Monitor .

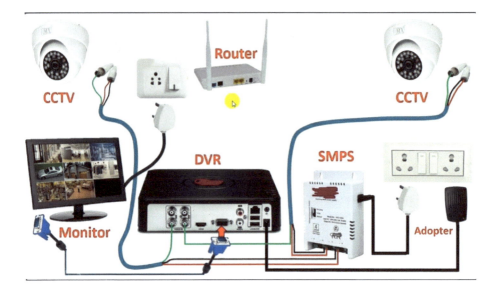

IP Camera Setup

Flow the Diagram & Connect Wire each other device as per previews guide chapters and plug-in electric socket for supply power on , if you every connation properly good within 2 Minute All Camera will be Live Show on your Monitor .

Chapter 9

Troubleshooting and Maintenance

- ° **Top 10 Common Hardware Related Problem & Solutions**
- ° **Top 10 Common Software Related Problem & Solution**
- ° **System Maintenance & Firmware and software updates**
- ° **Troubleshooting and Maintenance**
- ° **Top 10 Hardware Related Problem & Solution**

1. **What should I do if my CCTV camera has a blurry image?**

Clean the lens: Wipe the camera lens with a soft, clean cloth to remove any dirt or smudges.

Adjust the focus: If your camera has a focus ring, adjust it until the image is clear.

Check for obstructions: Ensure nothing is blocking the camera's view.

Check the camera resolution: Ensure the camera is set to the appropriate resolution for your monitor.

If Still Now Same Issue then All BNC & DC Connecter   Wash or Clean using Thinner Liquid , if Possible Change Connecter .

2.   What should I do if my CCTV camera Machine Always Beep Sound?

Check the HDD Working or Not .Maximum Time HDD Error Massage Show when Device Auto Restart .

Then You Have two Option to Resolve This Issue . (i) Remove Old Hard disk & Install New Hard disk As Per Your

Buauget . (ii) Go to Machine maintenance option find error Beep Disable option & Disable Hdd error Beep Option

And Restart Solve Issue But you Lost Your Recoding .

3 . What should I do if my CCTV camera has night vision issues?

Check the IR lights: Ensure the infrared (IR) lights on the camera are working.

Check for reflections: Remove any objects that might reflect IR light back into the camera.

Check the settings: Ensure the night vision mode is enabled in the camera settings.

Clean the lens: Make sure the camera lens is clean.

4. No Power to Camera

Error: Camera does not power on.

Troubleshooting Steps :

1. Check Power Source: Ensure the power outlet is working by plugging in another device

2. Inspect Power Adapter: Verify the adapter is properly connected and functioning.

3. Examine Power Cable: Look for cuts or damages in the cable.

4. Test with Multimeter: Use a multimeter to check for proper voltage.

5 . No Video Signal

Error: No video signal from the camera.

Troubleshooting Steps:

1. Check Connections: Ensure the video cable is securely connected to both the camera and the recorder/monitor.

2. Verify Video Format: Make sure the camera's video format matches the recorder's input (e.g., NTSC/PAL).

3. Inspect Cable: Test the cable with another camera to rule out damage.

4. Replace Camera: If other steps fail, the camera may be faulty.

6 . Interference Lines on Screen ?

Error : Horizontal or vertical lines on the screen.

Troubleshooting Steps :

1. Check Grounding: Ensure the system is properly grounded.

2. Inspect Cables: Replace or reroute cables to avoid interference.

3. Separate Power and Data Cables: Keep power and video cables separated.

4. Use Shielded Cables: Consider using shielded cables to reduce interference.

7 .No Audio Issues

Error: No audio from the camera.

Troubleshooting Steps:

1. Check Microphone: Ensure the camera has a built-in microphone.

2. Verify Connections: Check audio cable connections.

3. Enable Audio: Ensure audio recording is enabled in the settings.

4. Test with Another Device: Test the microphone with another recording device.

8. Camera Overheating

Error : Camera becomes too hot to touch.

Troubleshooting Steps:

1. Check Ventilation: Ensure proper ventilation around the camera.

2. Inspect Power Supply: Verify the camera is not receiving excessive voltage.

3. Relocate Camera: Move the camera to a cooler location.

4. Consult Manufacturer: Contact the manufacturer if overheating persists.

9. Wrong Time/Date

Error: Incorrect time/date on recordings.

Troubleshooting Steps:

1. Set Time Zone: Ensure the correct time zone is set in the settings.

2. Enable NTP: Use Network Time Protocol (NTP) for automatic time updates.

3. Manually Adjust Time: Set the time/date manually if necessary.

4. Check Battery: Ensure the internal clock battery is Charged or if Not Remove Old battery & Install New battery .

10. Limited Field of View

Error: Camera's view is too narrow.

Troubleshooting Steps:

1. Adjust Angle: Reposition the camera for a better angle.

2. Use Different Lens: Consider using a lens with a wider field of view.

3. Install Additional Cameras: Use multiple cameras to cover more area.

4. Remove Obstructions: Ensure no objects block the camera's view.

Top 10 Software Related Problem & Solution .

1. Why is my CCTV camera not recording?

Check the storage: Ensure there is enough space on the recording device (DVR/NVR/XVR).

Check the settings: Make sure the camera is set to record. Check the recording schedule and motion detection settings.

Check the cables: Ensure all cables are securely connected.

Check the power: Ensure the recording device is powered on.

2. Why is my CCTV camera not connecting to the network?

Check the network connection: Ensure the camera is connected to the network via Ethernet cable or Wi-Fi.

Check the IP address: Ensure the camera has a valid IP address and is not conflicting with other devices.

Check the router settings: Ensure the router is properly configured to allow the camera to connect.

Restart the camera and router: Sometimes, simply restarting the devices can solve connection issues.

3. What should I do if my CCTV camera has low video quality?

Check the resolution settings: Ensure the camera is set to the highest possible resolution.

Check the network bandwidth: If using a network camera, ensure your network can support high-quality video streaming.

Clean the lens: Ensure the camera lens is clean.

Check the lighting: Ensure the area being monitored has adequate lighting.

4. Why is my CCTV camera not detecting motion?

Check the motion detection settings: Ensure motion detection is enabled and properly configured.

Check the camera placement: Ensure the camera is positioned to cover the desired area.

Check for obstructions: Ensure nothing is blocking the camera's view.

Check the sensitivity settings: Adjust the sensitivity settings if the camera is not detecting motion accurately.

5 . Camera Not Detected by NVR .

Error: DVR/NVR cannot detect the camera.

Troubleshooting Steps:

1. Check Network Connection: Ensure the camera and NVR are on the same network its means IP Address proper.

2. Verify Camera Address: Ensure the camera's IP address is correct.

3. Update Firmware: Check for and install the latest firmware updates.

4. Restart Devices: Power cycles both the camera and the NVR.

6 . Motion Detection Not Working.

Error: Camera does not trigger motion alerts.

Troubleshooting Steps:

1. Enable Motion Detection: Verify that motion detection is enabled in the settings.

2. Adjust Sensitivity: Increase the sensitivity settings.

3. Check Detection Area: Ensure the motion detection area is correctly configured.

4. Test in Different Conditions: Test motion detection during different times of day.

7 . Storage Full

Error: DVR/NVR storage is full.

Troubleshooting Steps:

1. **Enable Overwrite:** Set the recorder to overwrite old recordings.

2. **Add Storage:** Install additional storage if possible.

3. **Review Recording Settings:** Adjust settings to lower resolution or frame rate.

4. **Backup and Delete:** Backup important footage and delete unnecessary files.

8 . Email Notifications Not Working

Error: No email alerts from the camera/DVR/NVR.

Troubleshooting Steps:

1. **Enable Email Alerts:** Ensure email notifications are enabled.

2. **Check Email Settings:** Verify the email server settings (SMTP, port, etc.).

3. **Test Email Account:** Test the email account settings by sending a test email.

4. **Check Spam Folder:** Ensure alert emails are not going to the spam folder.

9. Remote Viewing Not Working

Error: Cannot access the camera remotely.

Troubleshooting Steps:

1. **Enable Remote Access:** Ensure remote access is enabled in the settings.

2. **Check Port Forwarding:** Set up port forwarding on the router.

3. **Use Correct IP Address:** Verify the public IP address is correct.

4. **Update Software:** Ensure the remote viewing app/software is up to date.

10. Password Issues

Error: Forgot camera/DVR/NVR password.

Troubleshooting Steps:

1. Check Default Password: Refer to the user manual for default login credentials.

2. Reset Device: Perform a factory reset on the device.

3. Contact Support: Reach out to the manufacturer for password reset assistance.

4. Keep Passwords Secure: Store passwords securely to avoid future issues.

Common issues and their solutions
What should I do if my CCTV camera is not turning on?

Check the power supply: Make sure the power cable is securely connected to the camera and the power source.

Check the power outlet: Ensure the outlet is working by plugging in another device.

Check the power adapter: Ensure the adapter is functioning properly. You might need to use a different one to test.

Check the fuse: If your camera has a fuse, ensure it hasn't blown out.

Why is my CCTV camera showing a blank screen?

Check the video connection: Ensure the video cable is properly connected to the camera and the monitor.

Check the monitor: Test the monitor with another device to

make sure it is working.

Check the camera lens: Make sure there is no dirt or obstructions on the camera lens.

Check the camera settings: Verify the camera is on the correct input channel.

System maintenance & Firmware software updates

Troubleshooting Steps

1. Check Storage: Ensure there is enough storage space.

2. Verify Schedule: Ensure the recording schedule is correctly set.

3. Inspect Network: Ensure stable network connectivity for IP cameras.

Firmware software updates

Inspect Network : Ensure stable network connectivity DVR / NVR / XVR .

Update Firmware : if Your System Connect to Internet Then You Check Update if it Is found Update ,Then Install the latest firmware updates & Restart .

Equipment replacement and upgrades

Spacel basis Regular Check DVR / XVR Device All BNC & DC Cannter Wash or Clean using Thinner Liquid , if Posibal Yearly basise Change Connters .

Chapter 10

Basic of Marketing & Sales for Entrepreneur

- ◦ **Categorise of cities & Example**
- ◦ **Marketing & Sales Strategy**

- ◦ **Service After Sales**
- ◦ **Quotation Templates**
- ◦ **Billing Templates**
- ◦ **Basic guidance of AMC**

Basic Concept of Marketing & Sales for Entrepreneur

Introduction

Marketing and sales are critical components of a successful CCTV installation Business. Whether you're targeting urban or rural areas, having a robust strategy will help you reach your target market, generate leads, and convert those leads into loyal customers. This chapter will guide you through various marketing and sales strategies tailored for Tier-1, Tier-2, Tier-3 cities, and rural areas, providing you with the tools to establish and grow your Business.

Understanding Your Market (Categorise of Cities)

Before diving into specific strategies, it's essential to understand the unique characteristics of your target market. Here's a Breakdown of the different tiers and rural areas:

Tier-1 Cities: These are The Major Metropolitan Areas with a large population and higher income levels.

List of Tier-1 Cities:

1. Mumbai
2. Delhi
3. Bangalore
4. Chennai
5. Hyderabad
6. Kolkata
7. Pune

8. Ahmadabad

Marketing Strategies

Digital Marketing

1. SEO (Search Engine Optimization): Optimize your website to rank higher in search engine results. Use keywords like "CCTV installation in Kolkata and "best security cameras in Purulia".

2. PPC (Pay-Per-Click) Advertising: Invest in Google Ads and social media ads targeting specific demographics and locations.

3. Social Media Marketing: Use platforms like Facebook, Instagram, LinkedIn, and Twitter to engage with potential customers. Share success stories, customer testimonials, and informative content about CCTV systems.

Networking and Partnerships
1. Business Networking Events : Attend local business events and security industry conferences to build relationships with potential clients and partners.

2. Partnerships with Real Estate Developers : Collaborate with real estate developers and property management companies to offer bundled security solutions for new properties.

Content Marketing
1. Blogging : Create informative blog posts about the importance of security, CCTV technology advancements, and installation tips.

2. Video Tutorials : Produce videos demonstrating how to install and maintain CCTV systems, which can be shared on YouTube and social media.

Example Diagram: Digital Marketing Funnel for Tier-1 Cities
![Digital Marketing Funnel](https://i.imgur.com/8Kzxn4p.png)

Tier-2 Cities : These are smaller metropolitan areas or large cities that are not as economically developed as Tier-1 cities but still have significant growth potential.

List of Tier-2 Cities

1. Agra
2. Ajmer
3. Aligarh
4. Amravati
5. Amritsar
6. Asansol
7. Aurangabad
8. Bareilly
9. Belgaum
10. Bhavnagar
11. Bhiwandi
12. Bhopal
13. Bhubaneswar
14. Bikaner
15. Bilaspur
16. Bokaro Steel City
17. Chandigarh
18. Coimbatore
19. Cuttack
20. Dehradun
21. Dhanbad
22. Durg-Bhilai Nagar
23. Durgapur
24. Erode
25. Faridabad
26. Firozabad
27. Ghaziabad
28. Gorakhpur

29. Gulbarga
30. Guntur
31. Gwalior
32. Hubli-Dharwad
33. Indore
34. Jabalpur
35. Jaipur
36. Jalandhar
37. Jammu
38. Jamnagar
39. Jamshedpur
40. Jhansi
41. Jodhpur
42. Kannur
43. Kanpur
44. Kochi
45. Kolhapur
46. Kollam
47. Kota
48. Kozhikode
49. Kurnool
50. Ludhiana
51. Madurai
52. Malappuram
53. Mathura
54. Mangalore
55. Meerut
56. Moradabad
57. Mysore
58. Nagpur
59. Nanded
60. Nashik
61. Nellore
62. Noida
63. Patna
64. Pondicherry

65. Raipur
66. Rajkot
67. Ranchi
68. Rourkela
69. Salem
70. Sangli
71. Siliguri
72. Solapur
73. Srinagar
74. Surat
75. Thiruvananthapuram
76. Thrissur
77. Tiruchirappalli
78. Tirunelveli
79. Tiruppur
80. Ujjain
81. Vadodara
82. Varanasi
83. Vasai-Virar City
84. Vellore
85. Vijayawada
86. Visakhapatnam
87. Warangal

Community Engagement

1. Local Sponsorships: Sponsor local events, sports teams, or community programs to increase brand visibility.
2. Workshops and Seminars: Conduct security awareness workshops for residents and business owners.

Traditional Marketing

1. Local Newspapers and Magazines : Advertise in local print media to reach a broader audience.
2. Billboards and Flyers : Use billboards and distribute flyers in

high-traffic areas to attract attention.

 Referral Programs

1. Customer Referral Programs : Encourage satisfied customers to refer friends and family by offering discounts or rewards for successful referrals.
2. Partnerships with Local Businesses : Form alliances with local businesses such as hardware stores and security firms to cross-promote services.

Example Diagram: Community Engagement Strategy for Tier-2 Cities
![Community Engagement Strategy](https://i.imgur.com/QWJPCVb.png)

Tier-3 Cities : These are smaller cities or large towns with moderate population sizes and slower economic growth. Examples include smaller regional hubs and suburban areas.

List of Tier-3 Cities

1. Adoni
2. Agartala
3. Ahmednagar
4. Aizawl
5. Akola
6. Alappuzha
7. Alwar
8. Ambala
9. Anantapur
10. Arrah
11. Aurangabad
12. Bahraich
13. Ballari
14. Balurghat
15. Baranagar

16. Barasat
17. Bardhaman
18. Bharatpur
19. Bathinda
20. Bhagalpur
21. Bhilai Nagar
22. Bhiwani
23. Bidar
24. Bikaner
25. Bilaspur
26. Bongaigaon
27. Burhanpur
28. Cachar
29. Chandanagar
30. Chandrapur
31. Chhindwara
32. Chittaurgarh
33. Chittoor
34. Dibrugarh
35. Dimapur
36. Dindigul
37. Eluru
38. Faizabad
39. Gandhidham
40. Gangtok
41. Giridih
42. Gulbarga
43. Hapur
44. Haridwar
45. Hisar
46. Hoshiarpur
47. Hoshangabad
48. Jalgaon
49. Jalna
50. Jammu
51. Jamnagar

52. Jaunpur
53. Jhansi
54. Jind
55. Kakinada
56. Kalyan-Dombivali
57. Kannur
58. Karimnagar
59. Khammam
60. Kishanganj
61. Kolar
62. Kollam
63. Korba
64. Kottayam
65. Kumbakonam
66. Kurnool
67. Latur
68. Mandsaur
69. Mathura
70. Mirzapur
71. Nadiad
72. Nagercoil
73. Nagapattinam
74. Nanded
75. Nandyal
76. Nandurbar
77. Narsinghpur
78. Navsari
79. Neyveli
80. Ongole
81. Orai
82. Palakkad
83. Palwal
84. Pali
85. Panchkula
86. Panipat
87. Parbhani

88. Phagwara
89. Pithampur
90. Pollachi
91. Porbandar
92. Pudukkottai
93. Purnia
94. Rae Bareli
95. Rajapalayam
96. Rajgarh (Churu)
97. Rajnandgaon
98. Ramagundam
99. Ramgarh
100. Rampur
101. Ranaghat
102. Ratlam
103. Rewa
104. Rohtak
105. Roorkee
106. Sagar
107. Saharsa
108. Samastipur
109. Sambalpur
110. Sangli-Miraj & Kupwad
111. Satna
112. Shimla
113. Shimoga
114. Sikar
115. Silchar
116. Siliguri
117. Sitapur
118. Sivakasi
119. Sonipat
120. Srikakulam
121. Sultan Pur Majra
122. Suratgarh
123. Surendranagar

124. Thanjavur
125. Thoothukudi
126. Thrissur
127. Tiruchirappalli
128. Tirupati
129. Tirupur
130. Tiruvannamalai
131. Tumkur
132. Udaipur
133. Udupi
134. Ujjain
135. Unnao
136. Vaniyambadi
137. Vellore
138. Veraval
139. Vidisha
140. Vellore
141. Warangal
142. Yamunanagar
etc

Direct Marketing

1. **Cold Calling: Reach out to potential customers directly through phone calls.**
2. **Door-to-Door Marketing Visit homes and businesses to offer personalized consultations and free security assessments.**

Local Advertising

1. **Radio Ads : Advertise on local radio stations to reach a wider audience.**
2. **Community Bulletin Boards : Post advertisements on community boards in public places like libraries, community**

centers, and local stores.

Local Partnerships

1. Collaboration with Local Authorities : Work with local law enforcement and municipal authorities to promote the benefits of CCTV systems for community safety.
2. Real Estate Agents : Partner with local real estate agents to recommend your services to new homeowners.

Example Diagram: Direct Marketing Strategy for Tier-3 Cities
![Direct Marketing Strategy](https://i.imgur.com/XVpAb1X.png)

Rural Areas : These are regions with low population density and limited access to urban amenities. They often have different security needs and purchasing behaviours.

Rural Areas

Awareness Campaigns

1. Security Workshops : Conduct free workshops in rural communities to educate residents about the benefits of CCTV systems.
2. Demonstration Events : Host events where you demonstrate the installation and functionality of CCTV systems.

Word-of-Mouth Marketing

1. Local Influencers : Engage local community leaders and influencers to spread the word about your services.
2. Satisfied Customer Testimonials : Use testimonials from satisfied rural customers to build trust and credibility.

Local Advertising

1. Flyers and Posters: Distribute flyers and put up posters in local shops, post offices, and community centres.
2. Local Radio and TV: Advertise on local radio stations and TV channels that are popular in rural areas.

Example Diagram: Awareness Campaign Strategy for Rural Areas
![Awareness Campaign Strategy](https://i.imgur.com/kL6zjxp.png)

---

3. Sales Strategies

a. Sales Funnel

Lead Generation

1. Website Forms : Use contact forms on your website to capture leads.
2. Landing Pages : Create targeted landing pages for specific campaigns.

Lead Nurturing

1. Email Marketing : Send regular newsletters and promotional emails to keep potential customers engaged.
2. Follow-Up Calls : Make follow-up calls to leads who have shown interest in your services.

Closing the Sale

1. Personalized Consultations : Offer personalized consultations to understand the specific needs of the customer.
2. Custom Quotes : Provide custom quotes based on the consultation.

Post-Sale Service

1. **Customer Support:** Offer excellent customer support to resolve any issues.
2. **Maintenance Contracts:** Offer maintenance contracts to ensure long-term customer satisfaction.

Conclusion

Marketing and sales are integral to the success of your CCTV installation business. By understanding the reach and convert potential customers. Use the diagrams and strategies provided in this chapter to guide your efforts, and continually adapt to changing market conditions to ensure long-term success.

Project Quotation templates for Client

Invoice For After Successfully Project

Business Name
123 Street Address, City, State, Zip
Website, Email Address
Contact Number

invoice

LOGO

BILL TO

Person Name
Business Name
Address
Contact Number

SHIP TO

Person Name
Business Name
Address
Contact Number

Invoice Date: 11/11/11
Due Date: 12/12/12

DESCRIPTION	QTY	UNIT PRICE	TOTAL
			0.00
			0.00
			0.00
			0.00
			0.00
			0.00
			0.00
			0.00
			0.00
			0.00
			0.00
		SUBTOTAL	0.00
		DISCOUNT	0.00
		SUBTOTAL LESS DISCOUNT	0.00
		TAX RATE	0.00%
		TOTAL TAX	0.00
		SHIPPING/HANDLING	0.00

Thank you for your business!

Terms & Instructions

Balance Due ₹ -

Feedback Mail silicon.corporation20@gmail.com

Scan QR for Paid Support

www.ingramcontent.com/pod-product-compliance
Lightning Source LLC
Chambersburg PA
CBHW041152050326
40690CB00001B/446